MUSHROOMS

AND THEIR CULTIVATION.

A Handbook for Amateurs dealing with the Culture of Mushrooms in the Open-air, also in Sheds, Cellars, Greenhouses, etc., and the best methods of Cooking them; including a Description of other Edible Fungi.

BY

T. W. SANDERS, F.L.S.

(Knight of the First Class of the Royal Order of Wasa, Sweden ; Editor of "Amateur Gardening," etc.)

ILLUSTRATED.

Mushrooms

A mushroom (or toadstool) is the fleshy, spore-bearing fruiting body of a fungus, typically produced above ground on soil or on its food source. The standard for the name 'mushroom' is the cultivated white button mushroom, *Agaricus bisporus*; hence the word 'mushroom' is most often applied to those fungi (Basidiomycota, Agaricomycetes) that have a stem (stipe), a cap (pileus), and gills (lamellae, sing. lamella) or pores on the underside of the cap.

The terms 'mushroom' and 'toadstool' go back centuries and were never precisely defined, nor was there consensus on application. The term 'toadstool' was often, but not exclusively, applied to poisonous mushrooms or to those that have the classic umbrella-like cap-and-stem form. Between 1400 and 1600 AD, the terms *tadstoles, frogstooles, frogge stoles, tadstooles, tode stoles, toodys hatte, paddockstool, puddockstool, paddocstol, toadstoole, and paddockstooles* sometimes were used synonymously with *mushrum, muscheron, mousheroms, mussheron, or musserouns.* The term 'mushroom' and its variations may have been derived from the French word *mousseron* in reference to moss (*mousse*).

Identifying mushrooms requires a basic understanding of their macroscopic structure. Most are Basidiomycetes and gilled. Their spores, called basidiospores, are produced on the gills and fall in a fine rain of powder from under the caps as a result. As a result, for most mushrooms, if the cap is cut off and placed gill-side-down overnight, a powdery impression reflecting the shape of the gills (or pores, or spines, etc.) is formed (when the fruit body is sporulating). The colour of the powdery print, called a spore print, is used to help classify mushrooms and can help to identify them. Spore print colours include white (most common), brown, black, purple-brown, pink, yellow, and creamy, but almost never blue, green, or red.

While modern identification of mushrooms is quickly becoming molecular, the standard methods for identification are still used by most and have developed into a fine art, harking back to medieval times and the Victorian era. The presence of juices upon breaking, bruising reactions, odours, tastes, shades of colour, habitat, habit, and season are all considered by both amateur and professional mycologists. Tasting and smelling mushrooms carries its own hazards though, because of poisons and allergens. In general, identification to genus can often be accomplished in the field using a local mushroom guide. Identification to species, however, requires more effort; and one must remember that a mushroom develops from a button stage into a mature structure, and only the latter can provide certain characteristics needed for the identification of the species.

However, over-mature specimens lose features and cease producing spores. Many novices have mistaken humid water marks on paper for white spore prints, or discoloured paper from oozing liquids on lamella edges for coloured spore prints. A number of species of mushrooms are poisonous; although some resemble certain edible species, consuming them could be fatal. Eating mushrooms gathered in the wild is risky and should not be undertaken by individuals not knowledgeable in mushroom identification, unless the individuals limit themselves to a relatively small number of good edible species, that are visually distinctive. People who collect mushrooms for consumption are known as 'mycophagists', and the act of collecting them for such is known as mushroom hunting, or simply 'mushrooming'. Have fun!

EDIBLE TUBE MUSHROOM (Boletus edulis).

A truly delicious wild fungus. Common in oak woods in Autumn.
See Chap. XIV.

A FOREWORD.

This Handbook has been written to meet the requirements of amateur gardeners who need guidance as to the various methods of growing mushrooms for home consumption. Our aim has been to supply information in as concise and lucid a manner as possible on the culture of the mushroom on ridges or beds in the open air, in boxes and tubs in cellars, etc.; under greenhouse staging; in old hotbeds or in frames; also in pastures. No pains have been spared to make every phase of the art plain and easy to understand, in order that even the merest novice may follow with hope of certain success.

To render the volume of still greater value to the amateur we have not only instructed him how to grow mushrooms, but also how to cook them in various appetising ways. There is no vegetable so delicious as the mushroom, if properly cooked; and if the reader will only prepare the produce according to one of the recipes given, he will appreciate it to a far greater extent than he has hitherto done.

Then, we know there are many country readers who in summer and autumn come across a great number of fungi growing in woodland, upland, and mead, but are unaware of the fact that a large proportion of them are edible. The popular notion is that every fungus, except the true mushroom, is a "toadstool," and poisonous withal. It is true that a large number of fungi are highly poisonous, but this fact should not deter the reader from studying the various fungi that come under his observation, and gradually finding out those which are edible and those that are not.

To assist the country reader, therefore, to determine those that are safe to eat, we have supplied a chapter giving a brief description of the edible kinds, accompanied, as far as possible, with illustrations of them. Some of the so-called "toadstools" are most delicious, and highly appreciated by epicures who have proved their value as food products.

To enable readers of this volume to determine which are safe and which poisonous among our native fungi, we shall be most happy to receive specimens, securely packed in tin or wooden boxes, and report upon them in the pages of "Amateur Gardening."

Those who desire information on the culture of mushrooms for market will find the needful guidance in No. 4 Handbook, "Mushrooms, etc., for Profit," published at 1s. 2d., post free, at this office.

1909.   T. W. S.

CONTENTS.

Mushrooms and their Cultivation.

CHAPTER I.

HISTORICAL NOTES.

No mention is made of the Mushroom in Holy Writ, but there is no doubt that it was known to, and cultivated by, the ancients. History tells us, at any rate, that Columella. Pliny and Virgil made references to it in their writings before and just after the Christian era. Says Pliny (circa 23 to 79 A.D.): "The last device of our epicures to sharpen their appetites, and tempt them to eat inordinately, is the cooking of mushrooms." Later he remarks: "There are some dainty wantons of such fine taste, and who study their appetite to such an excess, that they dress mushrooms with their own hands, so that they may feed on the odour during the time they are handling and preparing this food, with their fine amber knives and silver vessels about them." We know, too, as a matter of history that Agrippina is supposed to have poisoned her husband, the Emperor Tiberius Claudius, by means of fungi.

Gerard and Lord Bacon allude to the Mushroom in their writings in the sixteenth century, but more in a derogatory than an appreciative spirit. Says Gerard: "Many wantons,

.hat dwell neer the sea, and have fish at will, are very desirous, for change of diet, to feede upon the birds of the mountaines; and such as dwell vpon the hills and champion grounds doe long after sea-fish; many that haue plenty of both doe hunger after the earthie excresences, called mushrooms: fewe of them are good to be eaten, and most of them doe suffocate and strangle the eater. Therefore I giue my simple auduice vnto those that loue such strange and newe fangled meates, to beware of licking honie among thornes, least the sweetness of the one do not counteruaile the sharpness and pricking of the other." Lord Bacon is equally quaint in his reference to the Mushroom. He says: "Mushrooms have two strange properties: the one that they yield so delicious a meate; the other, that they come up so hastily, as in a night, and yet are unsown; and therefore, such as are upstarts in state are called in reproach mushrooms. We find that mushrooms cause the accident we call Incubus, or the mare in the stomach; and therefore the surfeit of them may suffocate and empoyson, and this showeth that they are windy, and that their windiness is gross and swelling, not sharp and griping." These opinions clearly indicate that mushrooms were not appreciated a few centuries ago.

Stephen Switzer, a skilled gardener in the time of Queen Anne, seems to have been the first English author to deal with the culture of the Mushroom. The first book published solely devoted to the subject appeared in 1779 from the pen of John Abercrombie. It was entitled "The Garden Mushroom: Its Nature and Cultivation, exhibiting full and plain Directions for Producing this Desirable Plant in Perfection and Plenty." From this fact we may reasonably assume that a good deal of attention was being paid at that time to the Mushroom.

In the last century great strides were made in the cultivation of mushrooms. In all the larger type of gardens special structures were built expressly for growing them, and a more or less continuous supply was maintained by the skill of the gardener. The idea of growing mushrooms thus is recorded to be due to Oldacre, gardener to Sir Joseph

Banks, early in the last century, who either saw or heard of the method being practised in Germany.

Mushrooms were grown for Covent Garden fully fifty years ago, the chief supply in those days coming from a market gardener named Steel, of Fulham Fields, and Dancer, of Chiswick, districts then famous for market gardening, but now covered by bricks and mortar.

At the same period the French market gardeners were actively engaged in cultivating mushrooms in caves or disused quarries, and making quite a small fortune out of the industry. In due course the growth of mushrooms became more general in this country, and many misguided people conceived the idea that, as in the case of the French gardening industry, because it paid so well in France it would be bound to do so here. Everybody wanted to embark in mushroom growing a few years ago, but alas! few are now engaged in the industry on a large scale.

CHAPTER II.

MUSHROOM SPAWN.

THE primary essential in the cultivation of mushrooms is the "spawn." This may be obtained in a natural way or in the form of "bricks" from a seedsman. The last-named method is the one usually adopted, since the former requires a good deal of skill and expert knowledge to obtain the "spawn" in the right condition.

What is Spawn?—Spawn is the vegetative part of a fungus, that which gives birth to the Mushroom as we know it. Technically, it is called the mycelium, a substance consisting of white threads usually growing in a mass in manure.

These threads have the power of collecting and assimilating food, and are to the Mushroom what the roots and leaves are to a plant, the means of producing fruit and spores which are equivalent to seeds. The Mushroom—i.e., the part to eat—is merely the sporocarp, or fruit, of the mycelium which grows beneath the surface of the soil or manure. When a mushroom is fully grown and has begun to decay, millions of tiny bodies called spores escape from the gills, and are distributed around on the soil or wafted by the wind to other parts of the field or garden. Provided the conditions are congenial, the microscopic spores germinate and form the

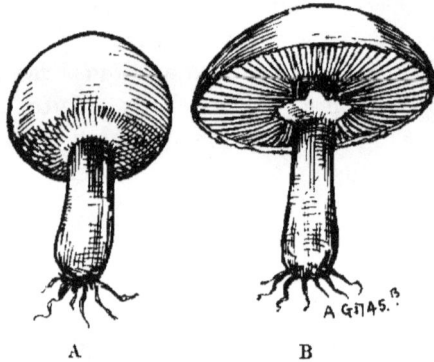

Types of Mushrooms.
A, "Button"; B, Fully Developed Mushroom.

white threads known as the mycelium. It is from the latter and not the former that the gardener looks to obtain his crop of mushrooms. The mycelium continues to grow and produce a crop of mushrooms, but no mushrooms appear directly as the result of the germination of the spores. Attempts have been made to germinate mushroom spores artificially, but all have so far failed to succeed. If it were possible to rear mycelium from spores we should obtain a more virile and productive spawn, and be able to grow much finer mushrooms than we now do. Such would be what is known as "virgin spawn," and be worth a goodly sum of money.

Formerly spawn was obtained from mill-tracks, where
horse droppings had been trodden into a hard mass by the
continued tramp of horses. In this dung spores doubtless
found their way, germinated, and produced the vigorous
mycelium known in days gone by as "mill-track or virgin
spawn." Nowadays mill-tracks are few and far between,
and the expert has to search for the mycelium in specially-
prepared manure, collect, and then preserve it in the special
form known as "bricks."

How to Make Spawn.—Those who for the first time
purchase mushroom spawn will, perhaps, be somewhat sur-
prised to discover that this is in the form of bricks, these
usually being 9in. long, 6in. wide, and 2in. thick. They are
made of a mixture of moist manure, pressed into moulds
much as common building bricks are made, and, on examination, one or more small circular patches of a different colour
to the rest will be found near the centre of each. These were
really fragments of good fresh spawn inserted while the
manure was moist, and the spawned bricks being duly
stacked thinly in a warm house soon became permeated by
the mycelium, the process being much the same as the
Israelites of old resorted to in leavening their dough.

All this seems simple enough, but the secret lies in doing
everything at the right time. Those who may feel disposed
to make the attempt must collect a heap consisting of two
parts cow dung, one part sheep droppings, and one part fine
loam; all to be well stirred together so as to become
thoroughly incorporated. It should then be spread out in
a dry, open shed on a hard level bottom, in a layer about
3in. thick, and well beaten down with a spade. When it
has dried somewhat, or has arrived in about the same state
as clay when made into bricks, all may be cut into 9in.
squares with a sharp, clean spade, two holes, 1½in. in diameter, being punched half through each, not far from the
centre, all being then piled with openings between them, or
pigeon-hole fashion, to dry. When quite dry the holes made
should be filled with new spawn, either collected from the

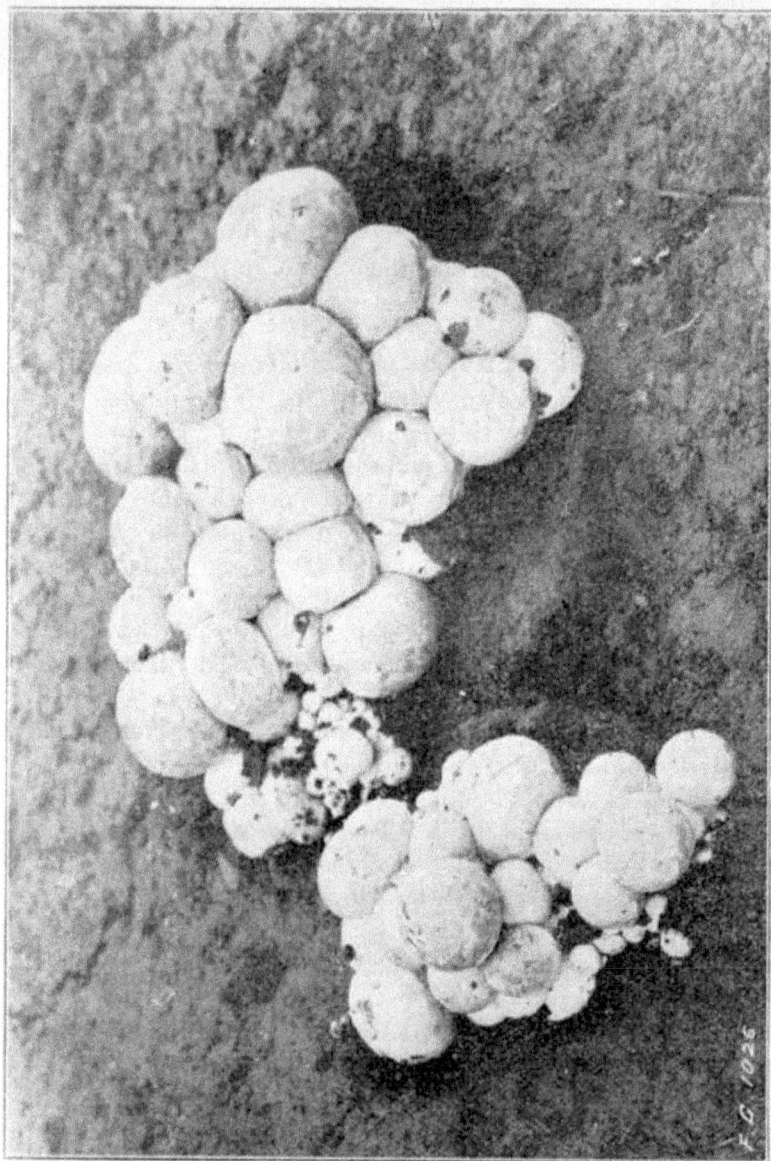

MUSHROOM (Agaricus campestris).

The growth of Mushrooms in clusters indicates the superior form of "spawn" used.

fields or taken from a temporarily spawned bed, and not
more than three weeks old, or found on the surface of old
beds.

The next proceeding is to store the spawned bricks thinly
in a warm, dry house, or, better still, in a frame over a
gentle hotbed. Sometimes the bricks are piled sparsely on a
heap of well-prepared stable manure in a shed, and covered
with more of the same, but a dry house or heated frame,
kept at a temperature of about 80 deg., is the safest. In
either case the bricks ought to be thoroughly permeated by
the manure in about a fortnight, and if, on being broken
open, they present a mouldy appearance, all should be
removed and stored thinly on edge, so as to keep quite dry,
in a room or dry shed till wanted for use.

French Spawn.—The French is very different in
appearance to the English spawn, as the former is supplied
in the form of mouldy flakes of strawy manure. It is sold
in neat deal boxes, and, as far as our experience goes, is not
equal to our own. Vendors of it make a mistake in not
supplying instructions in English instead of in their own, to
the majority of our countrymen, unintelligible jargon.

Another Method of Obtaining Spawn.—There
are other methods of increasing spawn which are worthy of
being tried, especially by those who are anxious to make
a profit of their beds. Some of the best spawn we ever used
was taken from an old melon bed, the sides or lining generally of which was spawned about the first week in August.
The heating material for all the beds—we had spawned
several—consisted of cow-yard and horse-stable manure in
about equal proportions, and, as a matter of course, well
mixed and prepared by several turnings before it was used
either for forming the hotbed or for subsequent linings.
When the crop of melons commenced to ripen off, at which
stage less water was given, the bed was spawned inside and
out, and without any further trouble any amount of flaky
manure well overrun by the mycelium was available both

for use and storing. We calculated we saved at least £2 by not having to purchase spawn, and the mushrooms we obtained were numerous and heavy. Hotbeds, formed with leaves and manure, all of which we must again allude to, would answer nearly or quite as well, pieces of brick spawn being about the size of a hen's egg, and inserted firmly 8in. apart in the sides of the hotbed. In any case the spawn or mycelium must not be allowed to reach the coarser stage previously alluded to before it is either used for spawning fresh beds or stored thinly on a dry shelf.

A Simple Method of Increasing Spawn on a small scale, and which might well be tried, consists merely of filling clean 6in. pots as firmly as possible with horse-droppings, prepared exactly the same as advised for flat beds,

A "BRICK" OF MUSHROOM SPAWN.

The lines indicate the division of the "brick" into twelve parts. Best results are obtained when the "brick" is divided into eight portions only.

in the centre of each being placed a small piece of brick or other spawn. The more solid the manure is rammed about the spawn the more readily the mycelium spreads. The pots should be set in a warm house, or in any dry position where the heat does not decline much below 60 deg. In from a fortnight to three weeks it will most probably be found, on turning out the contents of one of the pots, that the mycelium has spread through the manure, and the latter is therefore fit for spawning beds. If it cannot be used at once, the manure—or spawn, as it may now be termed—ought to be turned out of the pots and divided into good-sized lumps or flakes, and be kept cool and dry till needed. If kept too long in pots and heat it is soon spoilt for spawning purposes, but might produce a few mushrooms. The wisest course is to fill a few pots occasionally, or say about three weeks before a fresh bed will be ready to spawn. We have, by way of experiment, successfully used a mass of loamy soil turned out of pots in which old mushroom-bed manure had been used for covering the drainage crocks, and from this the mycelium spread into the soil.

Old Mushroom-bed Manure, mixed with a heap of decaying rubbish, manure, and soil for vegetable marrow beds, has repeatedly been the means of spawning a large open-air bed, the mushrooms being produced among the haulm of the plants overrunning the surface. We do not, however, advise anyone to depend upon the manure obtained from old beds for spawning new ones, as it is only those that have been kept rather drier than the rest in which the spores long survive.

Purchasing Spawn.—Spawn is usually sold by the bushel of sixteen bricks, each 9in. long, 6in. wide, and 2in. deep. The usual price is 5s. per bushel. In buying take great care to obtain it in a fresh condition, otherwise few, if any, mushrooms will appear. It can be had direct from the makers or through the medium of a seedsman, the former being the better mode of the two.

CHAPTER III

MANURES FOR BEDS.

Good manure is as essential as good spawn for successful mushroom culture. Too much care, in fact, cannot be exercised on this point.

Suitable Manures.—The most suitable manure for mushroom culture is horse droppings from a stable littered with straw. Such manure, however, must be avoided where horses are frequently "doctored" with medicine, or where carrots are fed to them. The ideal manure is that from horses which have been fed on corn and hay. This manure should consist of one-third droppings to two-thirds of short straw not exceeding 9in. in length, and such as has been well stained with urine. The longer portions should be placed on one side to dry for future coverings for the beds. Manure containing shavings should be avoided as likely to produce other fungi than mushrooms. Horse manure from stables littered with sawdust is said to answer fairly well, but certainly not so good as the droppings and short straw. Peat moss litter manure, too, has been successful for mushroom beds.

Preparing the Manure.—Any bed formed quite in the open should be ridge-shaped, and in this case a good portion of straw ought to be mixed with the horse droppings. The preference should be given to manure that has been made by horses in full work, and that are fed on hard food. This ought not to be thrown into a deep hole to ferment, and become dry and musty before being taken in hand; nor should it be allowed to become badly saturated by rain. If about three good cartloads of fairly fresh manure can be

MUSHROOMS FOR COOKING OR MAKING KETCHUP.

The "buttons" are best for cooking and the large ones for making ketchup or grilling.

had at one time, enough can be sorted from this to form a ridge-shaped bed about 8ft. long. Separate quite the longest straw from the manure, leaving only the short and stained, which may be equal to one-third or rather more of the bulk. Take good care of the longer straw, keeping it in the dry, if possible, to prevent heating. The manure selected for the beds must be thrown into a conical heap to commence fermentation, which it should do, unless too dry, in the course of three days. Before the centre becomes violently hot turn the heap inside out; in other words, the outside of the first heap is to form the centre of the second. Leave thus for another two days, when another turn should be given. This proceeding should be repeated about five times, the preparation occupying from ten days to a fortnight. Heavy rains should be warded off by means of either shutters, glazed frame-lights, or strips of corrugated iron.

Should the weather be dry, then the chances are the manure will become too dry to ferment properly, and will require to be gently moistened each time it is turned. It should be remembered that the object of all this careful preparation is to get rid of noxious gases without greatly impairing the heating properties of the manure. To suit mushrooms the latter must be both sweet and in a steadily-decaying state, a gentle, lasting, and not a violent rank heat being necessary. When a bed is formed of badly-prepared materials it is liable to overheat, and become dry and musty in the centre, and mushrooms will not grow in such stuff. Sometimes the manure, if not well prepared, overheats to such an extent after spawning takes place as to quite destroy the mycelium, this being another very frequent cause of partial or complete failure. For flat beds, these being formed under cover of some kind, rather more of the short, stained straw should be separated in the first instance, but in all other respects the preparation ought to be much the same.

Tree Leaves.—Although short horse-stable manure and droppings are preferable for mushroom beds generally, it has frequently been found that good results attend the use of leaves for mushroom beds, either in the late autumn or spring months. We have not tried them in, nor do we think them suitable for ridge-shaped beds, but have experimented with them at different times in cold sheds, mushroom-houses, and early vineries. In the autumn we rarely get sufficient manure to form as many beds as are required, and that first led to the use of leaves. We have tried them mixed in about equal quantities of droppings, also with two parts of leaves to one of manure, and beds have been formed principally of leaves, only about five inches of droppings being spread on the surface, and in each instance the crops obtained were fully as heavy and good as those grown with the aid of horse-manure only.

In January hotbeds of leaves and manure are frequently formed in early vineries, principally for the purpose of starting the vines, a few pot plants perhaps also being plunged in them. If these beds are duly spawned and soiled they quickly produce a quantity of mushrooms, not very heavy or succulent, it is true, but fully appreciated by those who purchase or eat them, all the same. Even the hotbeds in forcing houses on which melon and cucumber plants are growing may be spawned, the mushrooms later on coming up thickly among a variety of pot plants that may be set on trellissing, either resting on or supported over the bed.

In all cases where leaves are used these must be prepared much as advised in the case of horse droppings before being made into a bed. Fermentation sweetens them, and also insures the requisite forwardness of decay, nothing but sweet, slow-decaying matter being a favourable medium for the spread of spawn. Oak leaves are the best, but we have at times been obliged to use these in mixture with beech and less durable kinds.

When leaves are used the beds ought to be made rather deeper, or say 18in. deep at the back and 15in. at the front; but, as regards firmness, the time and method of spawning, and other details, the other treatment is exactly the same as advised for the orthodox horse-manure beds.

CHAPTER IV.

OUTDOOR CULTURE.

In the case of outdoor culture it is desirable that the beds should be of the ridge-shaped type. No other form of bed retains its heat so well, or can be so effectively protected against heavy rains, frosts, or snow. Once more let us strongly advise novices to prepare the manure thoroughly well before making it into a bed. When pressed together into a deep ridge imperfectly - prepared manure is liable to overheat, the centre of the bed attaining to a white heat. This gets rid of every particle of moisture, leaving the manure in a dry, musty state, totally unfit for the production of mushrooms. Ridge-shaped beds should be located in a well-drained and sheltered position, cold northerly winds in particular being kept away from them as much as possible. A hard bottom is also desirable.

Forming the Beds.—Commence operations by first staking or marking out a width of 30in., the length varying from 6ft. to 100ft. or more according to the quantity of manure available. If previous instructions have been well attended to, the strawy manure will have been well shaken out, no great flakes being tolerated. Form the bed in layers of not more than 18in. at a time, well beating and trampling the manure according as the work goes on. From the 30in. width at the bottom gradually taper the beds, so that when a height of 30in. is reached the width at the top will be only 6in. Slightly round off the top and dress down the sides and ends with a fork, so as to give them a neat thatch-like appearance. Next thrust a few strong sticks well into the centre of the beds. These are to be examined frequently, and should they become so very hot as to be quite unbear-

able when held in the palm of the hand, then the bed is
becoming too hot, and holes must be bored down through
the centre about 10in. apart, this being best done with the
aid of a pointed iron rod.   These holes will let off any excess
vapour and check overheating.

Spawning the Beds.—Not till the trial sticks denote
a heat of about 80 deg., or can be borne comfortably in the

A LESSON IN OUTDOOR MUSHROOM CULTURE.

Fig. 1 shows the preparation of the manure ; 2, Latter made up into the ridge-
shaped bed ; 3, Bed covered with litter prior to spawning ; 4, Method of spawning
the   bed ;   5,   Bed covered   with mats   to   keep. it warm ;   6,   "Button";
7, "Broiler" mushrooms.

hand, should the spawning be done, undue haste being liable
to end badly.   Good fresh spawn should be used, the bricks
being broken up into about eight lumps, these to be inserted not less than 8in. or more than 10in. apart each way,

the lower row commencing 6in. from the ground, and finishing off the same distance from the top. Do not bore holes for the spawn, as vapour is liable to collect to an injurious extent in them if not properly closed again. Open shallow holes in the manure with the left hand, and fix the lumps of spawn in these with the right hand, disposing them flat or smooth side outwards and almost level with the surface. The manure should be made quite firm about the lumps, and if the weather be cold or wet, straw over or otherwise protect the beds. A sudden change from cold weather to that which

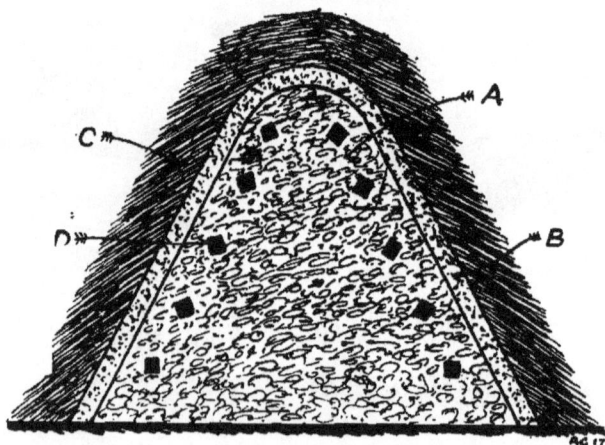

SECTION OF A RIDGE-SHAPED BED.
A, Manure; B, "Spawn"; C, Casing of soil;
D, Covering of long litter.

is warm and muggy is liable to cause a dangerous rise in the heat. Therefore examine the sticks once or twice daily, and if overheating is imminent again open the holes down through the centre of the beds.

Soiling the Beds.—If the beds are cased over with soil directly they are spawned there is all the greater likelihood of overheating taking place. Wait for three or four days, and, the heat then being only moderately high, the soil may be put on. The soil usually and rightly preferred is maiden loam, obtained from just under the turf in an old

MUSHROOM CULTURE IN LOW SPAN-ROOFED HOUSE.

Here is shown a bed made in a side border previously cropped with tomatoes. The surface of the bed is covered with dry leaves instead of litter.

F.G.1027.

pasture, this being passed through a half-inch sieve with a view to getting rid of lumps. Failing this, use the best loam or fresh soil procurable, ordinary garden soil obtained from just below the top spit frequently answering remarkably well. What will not do is soil that has been previously used for mushroom beds, nor any that is overrun by a fungus of any kind. We have frequently used the soil from old cucumber and melon beds with the best results, fine succulent Mushrooms in quantity being produced by its aid, whereas those obtained from very poor dry soil are not always so satisfactory. The whole of the bed should be covered with soil, beginning at the bottom as a matter of course, to a thickness of about 2in. after it is beaten down, a little less sufficing in the case of rather strong loams. It in a fairly moist state it will bind together sufficiently when well beaten with the back of a clean spade. There should be no watering and plastering of the soil, as this is inevitably followed by shrinkage and cracking, to the no small injury of the mycelium.

Covering the Beds.—Cover at first with a little of the strawy litter, and directly it is seen there is no likelihood of the beds overheating cover heavily with more of the same, a thickness of from 9in. to 12in. being desirable, disposing it in the form of a thatch, so as to throw off heavy rains. This covering of litter serves to prevent the rapid evaporation of the heat and moisture from the beds, and also excludes cold drying winds as well as strong sunshine. If these details are properly carried out nothing in the shape of watering ought to be needed to cause the beds to become productive, from four to six weeks being about the time that will elapse before many mushrooms will be forthcoming. Before much further advice concerning the treatment of these beds in the autumn and winter is needed it will, all being well, be forthcoming in these pages. At present we will only add that one or two more successional beds may well be formed and spawned at intervals of a fortnight or three weeks.

CHAPTER V.

INDOOR CULTURE.

THE month of September is a good time to form beds in out-
houses, disused stable stalls, and, in particular, those snug
thatched sheds often to be found in a corner near to a garden.
These latter are usually utilised for the storage of potatoes
and other roots and a variety of lumber. An equally suitable place might frequently be found for "ware" potatoes
or those to be eaten, and still better storage quarters might
easily be found for the seed or planting tubers, these keeping
best in lighter quarters. Much lumber might be burnt with
advantage, and with a very little contrivance room for one
or more good mushroom beds be found.

Forming the Beds.—The beds may be formed either
on the floor, being enclosed by the walls at the back and side
or sides and the front kept together by means of stout stakes
and boards not less than 1½in. in thickness and 14in. deep.
Strong benches with similar front boards are also suitable for
mushroom beds, and these in regular mushroom houses are
to be seen one above another, good head-room between them
only being needed. Sheds with open fronts may be turned to
good account for mushroom beds, only in this case more
protection from cold winds must be afforded. Sufficient
manure having been prepared, as previously advised, spread
a good layer of this over the bottom of enclosure, and either
well trample it or beat it down with a mallet or back of fork.
Then add other layers, and beat or trample them down as
before, eventually finishing off with a depth of 12in. in front
and 15in. at the back, leaving it in a smooth, solid state.
Thrust two or more trial sticks into the bed, examine frequently, and spawn when the heat stands at about 80 deg.,

or, to avoid repetition, when in much the same state as advised in the case of ridge-shaped beds. If from any cause the manure becomes too dry to ferment properly, it may become necessary to break up the bed and re-form it after the manure has had a gentle watering. An expert would not use very dry manure in the first place, but would give a gentle watering according as it is put together. If, on the other hand, the manure be in a wet state, moisture oozing out when a handful is squeezed, then some dry soil—or, better still, some peat moss litter—ought to be mixed with it.

Spawning the Bed.—Test the temperature of the manure by thrusting sticks in here and there in the beds

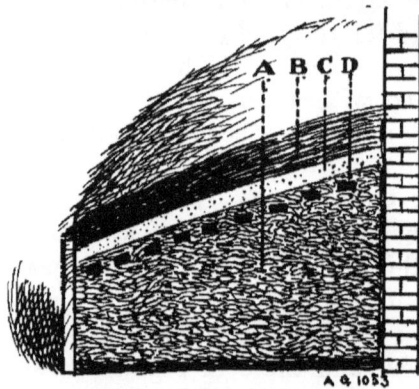

SECTION OF INDOOR BED.

The bed in this case is made against the wall. A, Shows the manure; B, The "Spawn"; C, Covering of soil; D, Surfacing of litter.

and withdrawing them occasionally to ascertain the progress of the heat. If the sticks feel very hot the temperature is too high; if comfortably warm it is right, and then the spawn should be inserted at once. A far safer way of ascertaining the temperature is to use a plunge thermometer. This, inserted in the bed, will give the exact temperature, which should be 80 deg. for the safe insertion of the spawn. Now obtain the bricks of spawn, divide each one into eight parts, and insert them 8in. apart each way. Make a cavity for each by means of the hand, as advised in Chapter IV.

Soiling the Beds.—The beds are ready for soiling about three days after spawning. Procure good loam, if possible, and pass through a half-inch sieve; then apply 2in. of it to the surface of the bed and beat it down firmly. After soiling cover with about 1ft. of straw or hay litter. See chapter on " Watering " for further details.

Temperature for Indoor Beds.—Some few readers may have the convenience of a heated structure for growing mushrooms in, and these are warned to be sparing of the fire heat. Only enough should be turned on to keep the temperature at about 50 deg., and this will only be needed when there are no fresh beds in the house, these latter affecting the heat considerably. We do not assert that another five degrees would do harm, but the best mushrooms are obtained in the temperature recommended, an occasional drop to 45 deg. doing no injury. As a matter of fact, it is only during the coldest weather that beds in sheds and other unheated places stop producing for a time. The walls and floors in heated houses should be syringed once or twice a day, but, as before hinted, care must be taken not to moisten the beds unduly.

CHAPTER VI.

CULTURE IN CELLARS.

STRICTLY speaking, no beds ought to be formed in cellars under occupied houses, but many worse things than these are frequently overlooked by the sanitary inspectors in both towns and villages. The genial warmth and humid atmosphere of a cellar suit mushrooms admirably, and that is why such immense quantities are grown in a variety of underground chambers in the neighbourhood of Paris, railway tunnels, and even arches under these and other raised roads also being utilised in this country. Mushroom-bed manure is scarcely what we should venture to take through a house into the cellar, for reasons that need not be given to married men; but there are many cellars that can be approached from the outside, area cellars also being very numerous.

The Beds.—If fairly large beds can be made in these then the fronts should be supported by boards and strong uprights, such as advised in the case of beds in sheds of various kinds. The other details also to be similar. In many cases the difficulty of having to carry manure in a cleanly manner through the passages of the house can be dispensed with by utilising old wine cases, a variety of other lighter and cheaper cases, boxes, and even strong hampers in which to form miniature beds. Excellent crops are sometimes had in this simple manner, and that, too, by people who could not well go in for mushroom culture on a larger scale. The manure used should be duly fermented and turned, but will scarcely require quite so long a period of preparation, small bodies of manure being less liable to overheat than larger masses. It should be a dark brown in colour, and only just moist enough to hold together when squeezed in the hand. If moisture squeezes out of it then it is too wet, and must be dried somewhat before it is used. Manure to the depth of from 12in. to 15in. is ample, and this should be made very firm, being well rammed, according as each layer is added.

Inserting the Spawn.—Directly a gentle heat has risen—or, say, in the course of three or four days—the spawning should be done. Break the bricks of spawn into lumps near the size of a hen's egg, and insert these just below the surface, and about 5in. apart all over the bed.

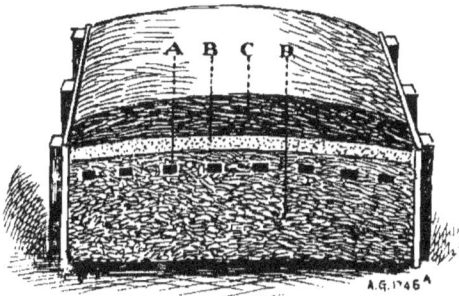

AN INDOOR BED.

A bed made on the floor of a cellar or shed. The sides are formed of planks and stout stakes. A is the "Spawn;" B, Covering of soil; C, Litter; D, The manure.

Cover with 2in. of good fine loam in about one week after spawning. All this work may be done before the boxes or baskets are taken into the cellar, but, according to our experience, the spawn runs best in the comfortable atmosphere of a cellar.

General Hints.—The bed, boxes, etc., should be covered with strawy litter, and the cellar kept as dark as possible. In the event of the bed becoming dry on the surface, remove the litter and give enough tepid water to just moisten the surface; then replace the litter. In about two months from spawning mushrooms will begin to appear.

CHAPTER VII.

CULTURE IN GREENHOUSES.

VERY few amateurs, and not many gardeners in charge of
small places, have the advantage of a snug, heated mushroom house proper, not a few also being unable or unwilling
to commence forming ridge-shaped beds. As we have
pointed out elsewhere, there are other ways of growing
mushrooms open to those willing to try them. The beds in
all unheated places other than warm cellars are almost certain to fail for a time, at any rate, during cold, frosty
weather, and that is where those who have the assistance of
heated quarters get the advantage. Now we have repeatedly
proved that a greenhouse, the temperature of which seldom
falls below 40 deg. and is generally kept somewhere near
45 deg. by night and from 5 to 10 deg. higher in the day-
time, will grow mushrooms well, and that, too, without de-
triment to the other contents of the house. It is the spaces
under both central and side stages that ought in many cases
to be chosen as sites for mushroom beds; and if a bed was
formed and spawned early in October, and another one three
weeks or a month later, a good succession of mushrooms
ought to be forthcoming from the middle of November till
March.

Forming the Beds.—What is wanted is a few stout
boards and strong stakes to form the fronts in the case of
the side beds, and both sides and ends when beds are to be
formed under the central stage. A depth of from 15in. to
18in. is suitable, and provision should be made in the shape
of either shutters or strips of corrugated iron for warding
off drips from pot plants overhead. Not a little depends
upon the proper preparation of the manure, so many err

in putting it together in a too dry state during a dry time, or in too wet a condition after a spell of rain. Hints on the proper method of preparing the manure will be found in Chapter III., the only difference being that all the long straw and the greater portion of that which is short and stained should be thrown out. When the centre of the heap

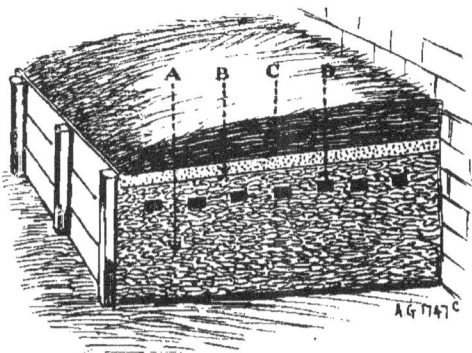

BED UNDER A GREENHOUSE STAGE.

A, Manure ; B, Soil ; C, Litter ; D, The "Spawn."

is no longer violently hot, and before it begins to feel cool, all rank smell being also got rid of, then is the time to form it into a bed.

Cultural Details.—These are precisely the same as advised in Chapter V. for indoor beds. The only other point to observe is the necessity of thoroughly excluding the light and paying attention to careful watering.

CHAPTER VIII.

SIMPLE METHODS.

In addition to the generally recognised methods described in preceding chapters, there are other simple ones which may interest the amateur gardener.

In Pots, Boxes.—Mushrooms may be grown in pots, boxes, or hampers. Taking boxes as most suitable, they should be about 3ft. long, 1½ft. broad, and 7in. deep. The first operation is to half-fill each with fresh horse-manure from the stables—the fresher the better—but if wet it should be allowed to dry for three or four days before being used. When placed in the boxes it should be well beaten down. In two or three days, if the manure has commenced to generate heat, the spawn may be inserted. Break each brick of mushroom spawn (which may be obtained from any seeds-man) into pieces 3in. square, lay these about 4in. apart on the surface of the manure, and allow them to remain for about six days. At the end of this time it will probably be found that the under side of the spawn has begun to run in the manure below; this being the case, place one and a-half inches of fresh manure on the top of the spawn, and beat it down, as in the first instance. In about a week, when you find that the spawn has run through the manure, the boxes will be ready to receive the soil. This should be placed two and a-half inches deep on the surface of the manure, and be beaten down thoroughly. When finished, the surface should be left quite smooth. In the space of five or six weeks the mushrooms will begin to show themselves, when, if the soil seems dry, a gentle watering with lukewarm water may be given. If the boxes are kept in a dark place, with an even temperature, and protected from the rays of the sun, the cultivator need not despair of producing a good supply of mushrooms during the summer months.

In Cucumber and Marrow Beds.—When the vegetable marrows and ridge cucumbers are grown on great heaps of decaying vegetable matter of various kinds, these, if spawned in July, or during the early part of August, not infrequently produce large crops of mushrooms late in the autumn. Much, however, depends upon the weather experienced, but if the month of August prove hot and dry, and September moderately so, the spawn spreads rapidly, and gentle autumn rains cause large clusters

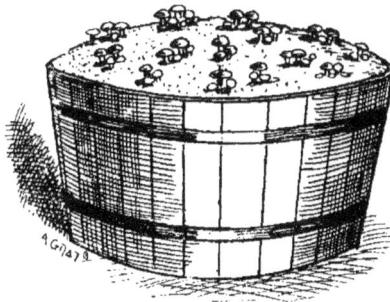

MUSHROOMS IN A TUB.

A simple way of growing Mushrooms in a cellar or outhouse.

of succulent mushrooms to come to the surface. When frosts destroy the marrow haulm, this should be carefully cut away, and the thick covering of strawy litter placed over the bed.

Beds of Mixed Soil and Manure.— Where there are no convenient spots in which to prepare the manure for the beds, the plan of mixing fresh, dry soil with quite fresh horse droppings ought to be tried. It is also worthy of a trial even when facilities exist for all work connected with mushroom culture. The dry soil absorbs ammonia, prevents overheating, and this admits therefore of beds being made up quickly, and, let us add, with every prospect of ultimate success. There must be no mistake about the mixing being thorough, and it may be done in this way: Spread the manure on the floor of a shed, and place fine soil on the top of this, in order to increase the bulk by another one-fourth, and then turn and mix all up into a heap. The beds should be made not more than 12in. in depth, and **duly spawned** when it is found, by the aid of trial sticks kept plunged in it, that the heat has declined so as to admit of the heated end being comfortably borne in the palm of the hand. In all other respects also treat similarly in the manner advised for other flat beds. When fine, dry

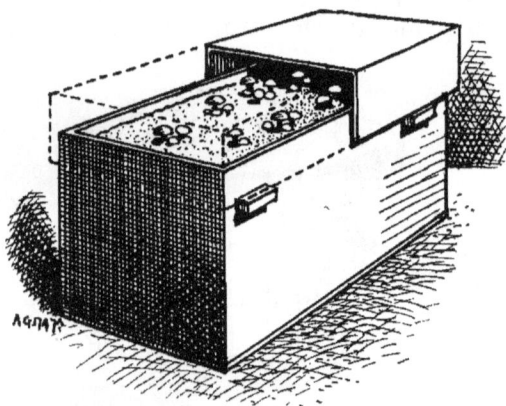

MUSHROOMS IN A BOX.

Another simple method of growing Mushrooms in a box or old packing case. The dotted lines show the remainder of the lid used for excluding light.

soil is thus mixed with the manure there is no rapid fermentation and very little smell noticeable, and owners of cellars should therefore give the plan a trial. When manure, or rather horse droppings, are scarce, and yet a fairly large bed is wanted, these may well be supplemented with oak or beech leaves. These should be thrown into a heap to heat, being turned three or four times during the course of a fortnight. They will be then decaying steadily, and may either have horse droppings mixed with them, or, better still, be made to form the foundation of a bed, a surfacing of prepared horse droppings, or even a layer from 4in. to 6in.

deep of good decayed manure being spread over it. There ought to be a depth of not less than 18in. of well-trampled leaves, which will then supply a lasting, steady, and sweet heat, the manure providing the suitable food for the mushrooms. Spawn, soil, and otherwise treat as advised in the case of other flat beds.

In Pastures, etc.—"It may not," says a correspondent in "Amateur Gardening," "be generally known that anyone can grow a good crop of mushrooms throughout the summer without any difficulty whatever. Those readers, for instance, who possess a meadow or a piece of grass land may lift square pieces of turf a foot or so in diameter, and dig out the soil to the depth of 9in. or 12in. Then fill in with freshly-gathered horse manure—that from the stable being best—and press this very firm, previously inserting two or three small pieces of mushroom spawn about 2in. below the surface. Replace the turf and beat it down with a spade. Pieces of spawn inserted thus, in clumps about a few yards from each other, will in a fine summer yield an immense quantity of mushrooms. It is not everyone, however, who has a meadow, and therefore some other plan must be adopted. Well, a good one is to insert pieces of spawn in the manure just below the surface, when making a hotbed for growing cucumbers or vegetable marrows. In celery trenches the writer has also inserted mushroom spawn with good results, and no doubt other readers could do likewise were they so disposed. It depends on the summer, however, as to whether plenty of mushrooms will be produced."

Mushrooms in Flower Bed.—"In a flat bed in my garden," remarks a correspondent in "Amateur Gardening," "about 6ft. by 4ft., a few mushrooms sprang up spontaneously, which prompted me to get a brick of spawn, which I broke into small pieces, then, with a pointed stick, made holes both in sides and top about 6in. deep, and inserted some in each, and made up the holes with the old rotten bed. In due course mushrooms began to appear; in three days I gathered thirty beautiful mushrooms from 1½in. to 3in. in diameter."

Mushrooms in Grass Plot.—"On May 23 I had," says a writer in "Amateur Gardening," "seven pieces of turf 1ft. square taken up in my grass plot, and 7in. depth of soil taken out, then filled with fresh horse manure rammed well down, and pieces of spawn inserted. Now, September 1, mushrooms are coming freely."

CHAPTER IX.

MUSHROOMS IN ODD CORNERS.

THE following hints and sketch originally appeared in "Amateur Gardening" from the pen of a valued contributor ("F. W."):

Apart from the cultivation of mushrooms as a commercial enterprise, it is also a most interesting hobby for gardening amateurs to pursue. Many readers may consider the Mushroom an unimportant subject, but, if they think for a moment of the immense consumption of this fungus in England and France alone, they will see that it is a matter worthy of consideration. There are growers of mushrooms in the suburbs of Paris who send to market more than 2,000lb. a day each. Then there is something almost wonderful about mushroom culture. No seeds are planted—only a few pieces of dirt apparently are put into a bed of manure, and yet a crop of pearly-white mushrooms is produced as if by magic.

The Mushroom is of an accommodating nature, and good crops may often be seen growing in old tubs in out-of-the-way corners of sheds and outbuildings, in abandoned greenhouses, and even on shelves in stables. If no accommodation of this description is available mushrooms may be grown in a back kitchen or cellar at home. All that is needed is a temperature of from 45 to 50 deg., some fresh horse manure, a quantity of loamy soil, and a few "bricks" of mushroom spawn from a reliable source.

The accompanying sketches are intended to illustrate

MUSHROOM CULTURE IN A ROOM AND ON THE LAWN.

Mushrooms may be grown in the cupboard of a disused room as shown at Fig. 1. Under a table as at Fig 2, if light be excluded. In a large pot or margarine tub, as at Fig. 3; or in the turf of the lawn as at Fig 5. Fig. 4 illustrates the details of Fig. 1. A, is the soil; B, The "Spawn;" C, The manure.

mushroom growing on a small scale—a multum-in-parvo method, in fact.

Multum-in-Parvo Beds.—Fig. 1 shows how mushrooms may be cultivated in the cupboard of a back kitchen if a good-sized wooden box or packing case is available. In

Fig. 2 mushrooms may be seen growing underneath a kitchen table, while the next sketch (Fig. 3) shows how an old bucket can be utilised for the culture of these edible fungi. Having procured what horse manure is needed for filling boxes or other receptacles, it should be forked over, removing any long straw litter in the process. It should then be thrown into a heap and allowed to remain for about three days. If well shaken out with a fork after this the material will become purified and lose its objectionable smell. The filling and spawning process connected with the culture of mushrooms in boxes is illustrated in Fig. 4. C is a mass of manure which has been trodden down in the box. The pieces of mushroom spawn inserted in the manure are marked B. and the top coating of loamy soil is indicated by A. In preparing the manure care must be taken that it does not get saturated by rain. When the manure has been placed in a box and become somewhat warm through fermentation, the proper time for spawning has arrived. The bricks of spawn should each be broken into eight large pieces, and these can be firmly pressed about 6in. apart into the manure. After that the miniature mushroom bed must be surfaced to the depth of half-an-inch with good turfy loam, chopped rather small, and beaten down moderately firm with the back of a spade. No watering or damping will be necessary unless this surface soil shows signs of drying to the extent of cracking, which must be avoided, as the threads of mycelium, or roots of the mushrooms, are broken, when fissures are caused in the soil by dryness. Mushrooms are often grown in entire darkness, and the crop should be ready in from six to eight weeks after the spawn has been inserted. When gathering mushrooms they should be gently pulled, not cut, as the base of the stems, if left, would rot, and cause other portions of the crop, not yet fit for gathering, to damp off.

Fig. 5 illustrates a method of growing mushrooms on a lawn, the turves being carefully lifted and replaced after pieces of spawn have been inserted two inches deep.

CHAPTER X.

WATERING MUSHROOM BEDS.

MANY amateurs, and also professional gardeners, take every pains in the preparation of the manure and formation of beds only to spoil everything by being over-zealous with the syringe or watering-pot. Moisture should always accompany fire heat when applied to mushrooms, but it ought to be in the atmosphere, syringing the beds heavily every day soon causing them to become very wet, and cold and saturation is quickly fatal to mushroom spawn. Too much water is also responsible for the failure of innumerable small mushrooms to attain a serviceable size. They may grow to near the size of small marbles only to disappoint by turning soft and brown.

Outdoor Beds.—When once a bed becomes very wet and cold it is not likely to be ever productive, and we would therefore strongly advise readers to ward off heavy rains from open-air beds by means of a heavy covering of dry strawy litter, a tarpaulin, or waterproof covering of some kind, or even thick carpet and stout canvas, being fastened securely over this during very rainy times. According to our experience open-air beds rarely need watering, especially after September. If, however, they are found in a dry state after being spawned from five to six weeks, few or no mushrooms showing at that time, then remove nearly all of the straw covering, and give a gentle yet thorough watering, using tepid water and a pot with a moderately fine rose on it. One watering may not prove sufficient to moisten both the soil and manure well, and in this case the dose should be repeated next day. Prior to re-covering the bed heavily with dry strawy litter, remove that which was left on the surface when the watering was done, and substitute dry soft litter. We advise leaving this thin covering

ORANGE-MILK MUSHROOM (Lactarius deliciosus).

An edible species which exudes an orange-coloured milky juice when cut or
bruised. Grows in fir woods.

by way of an aid to soaking the bed, and its removal afterwards because it is apt to cling too closely to the soil, thereby conducting warmth and moisture from the bed (which dry litter will not do), also favouring the spread of mould or destructive fungoid growths. When at any time, later on, the litter next the soil is found wet and cold, carefully remove it at once, for similar reasons to those just given, replacing with fresh dry litter. Never be chary of using strawy litter by way of a covering, a thickness of 12in. being none too much during the cold autumn and winter months.

In many cases the beds will commence producing mushrooms in quantity in about six weeks from the date of spawning without being watered; but if watering be necessary the crops will be a little later, though probably, if all goes on well, somewhat heavier. Only one person ought to attend to the gathering of the crops, constantly exposing all parts of the beds unnecessarily being a great mistake.

Indoor Beds.—In all other cases—that is to say, whether the beds are covered with frames or are in sheds, stables, cellars, and such like, or are on a small scale in boxes and hampers—there must be a period of not less than a month for the spawn to spread through the manure and soil, the best results being obtained when the beds are constantly warm, consequent upon the very steady decay of the manure, and only just moist. It will have been observed that extraordinary crops of mushrooms are obtained from the open fields after a fairly long period of dry, hot weather. While the latter lasts the mycelium is spreading, and it only needs a heavy downfall of rain to bring up the mushrooms. Too much moisture is, then, fatal to the spawn, as well as to the crops, after these have commenced forming; while dryness, though favourable to the spread of the mycelium, or very fine cottony threads that should be found spreading in all directions within a week or so of spawning, must be corrected before full crops will be obtained. Wait, therefore, for a month—or, better still, five weeks—before probing the beds very lightly at two or three places with a view to testing the state of the manure. If the latter is fairly moist, then wait patiently another fortnight, and unless the weather is very cold mushrooms most probably will be coming up very thickly in all directions. On the other hand, if the bed is found to be very dry, give one or two gentle waterings, as advised in the case of ridge-shaped beds, mulch with fresh strawy litter, and await results.

A lack of patience has been the cause of many failures. For instance, beds spawned late in October or early in November may fail to produce mushrooms before February or March. We have had exceptionally heavy crops from late-spawned beds that were not watered or forced in any way, and which were badly frosted during the winter.

CHAPTER XI.

USEFUL DATA.

THE following interesting items of information may be useful to mushroom growers:

Gathering Mushrooms.—It may, perhaps, be thought that no advice can be needed as to the gathering of the crops. "Any fool could do that simple job," will be the mental ejaculation, and so he or she could, but more depends upon the removal of mushrooms being done properly than the novice is aware of. In the first place, they must not be cut off. The old stumps, if left in the bed, are a source of danger to the rest of the crop, as they decay quickly, and the mould spreads from them in all directions, this effectually killing all young mushrooms it comes into contact with. Solitary mushrooms ought, then, to be pulled cleanly out of the bed, while in the case of clumps the more forward may be twisted off, and the remainder, with the solid conglomeration of stems in the soil, be cleanly scooped out. This will leave a fairly large hole, which should be filled with fresh loamy soil kept in readiness for this purpose. When this is done there is every likelihood of the broken thread-like roots left in the beds producing an abundant second crop of mushrooms. Pulling up the roots may mean the loosening or removal of a few small mushrooms, or "buttons," as they are termed, but all cooks and housewives can usually put these to a good use, and in any case it is a mistake to leave the stumps in the bed.

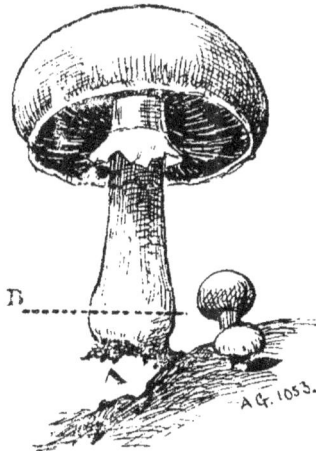

How to Gather Mushrooms.

As explained in accompanying paragraph, Mushrooms should be gathered by pulling them out of the bed as shown at A, not by cutting the stems through, as indicated by dotted line B.

Exhausted Beds.—When the first crop is about finished it does not follow that the bed is of no further value as far as mushroom growing is concerned; but, on the contrary, another good succession should be obtained. In most instances an examination of the bed after cropping ceases will disclose the fact that it is very dry, and our word may be taken as to its also being exhausted of much of its fertility. Now mushrooms must have good living, or quite as

much so as many vegetables, by far the most succulent produce being obtained when liquid manure of some kind has
been applied to partially-exhausted beds. After the first
crop has been cleared off give the bed a good soaking of
liquid manure—such, for instance, as well-diluted drainings
from a farmyard, or that obtained by soaking a bag of
sheep's droppings, cow manure, and horse droppings for
about a week in a tub of water, diluting this freely with
water when using it. Artificial manures may be substi-
tuted for either of the foregoing, and water impregnated
with salt at the rate of two ounces of the latter to one
gallon of the former, answers remarkably well. In either
case the water or liquid manure should be in a warm state,
or heated, say, to about 90 deg. when used. Give enough
at two or three times, if need be, to moisten the bed
thoroughly; then mulch with soft strawy litter, and look out
for more mushrooms in quantity shortly. It is the beds in
dry positions and in boxes and hampers that dry the quickest
and require the most attention.

Quantity of Manure to Make a Bed.—One ton
of manure will be required for every 4ft. run of ridge-shaped
bed, and a similar quantity for 6ft. run of flat bed.

Yield of Mushrooms.—Each lineal yard of a pro-
perly-prepared ridge-shaped bed should produce 20 to 25lb.
of Mushrooms.

Law in Relation to Field-grown Mushrooms.
—To protect mushrooms grown in fields from thieves, and to
secure a conviction in case of the latter being caught gathering
them, place a board up in the field containing the following
notice: "Mushrooms Cultivated Here." Salt should be
occasionally strewn over the field and spawn inserted, then
there will be ample justification for stating that mushrooms
are cultivated, and anyone caught gathering them may be
prosecuted for theft, as well as trespass. In the event of no
notice being exhibited in a field in which mushrooms are
grown naturally, the only remedy against a person gathering
them is a prosecution for trespass.

Expansive Power of Fungi.—Some fungi possess enormous expansive power during growth. At Basingstoke many years ago a paving stone weighing 83lb. was lifted off its bed by fungi growing beneath. The late Sir Joseph Banks records an instance of a wine cask leaking and providing food for the growth of fungi beneath. So great was the expansive power of the latter that it pushed the cask upwards to the roof of the cellar.

Fungi Poisoning.—In the event of anyone being taken suddenly ill through partaking of fungi in mistake for the Mushroom, prompt action should be taken at once. Mix two or three teaspoonfuls of mustard in half a pint of warm water, and administer it to the patient to cause immediate vomiting and the expulsion of the fungi from the stomach. When this has been accomplished give the patient a cup of strong coffee or tea. Even if a medical man be sent for the emetic recommended should without a moment's delay be administered.

Analyses of Fungi.—The following analyses of the food constituents of mushrooms, morels, and truffles appear in Kensington's "Composition of Foods, etc." (J. and A. Churchill):

Constituents.	Mushroom.	Morelle.	White Truffle.	Black Truffle.
Nitrogenous matter and sulphur	4·680	4.40	9·958	⟨8·755
Fatty matters ...	·396	·56	·442	·560⟩
Cellulose, dextrin, and other nitrogenous substances	3·456	3·68	15·158	⟨16·585
Mineral matters	·458	1·36	2·1(2	2·070⟩
Water	91·010	90·00	72·340	72·000
	100·000	100·000	100 000	100·990

A Mushroom House.—While, as explained in previous chapters, the Mushroom may be grown outdoors or in

cellars, sheds, or disused rooms, yet, where a regular supply
is required all the year round, a special structure is desired.
The usual type of mushroom-house is a span roof built on
the north side of a wall. The average width is about 10ft.,
a 3ft. path going down the centre, and a bed 3½ft. wide on
each side. The height of the back should be about 9ft. to
10ft., and the front 6ft. to 7ft. Both the side and end walls
should be built of 9in. brickwork. No windows or ventila-
tors will be required. There should, of course, be a 3ft.
doorway at one end. The roof is best composed of thatch
or heather, on account of keeping the interior cool in summer

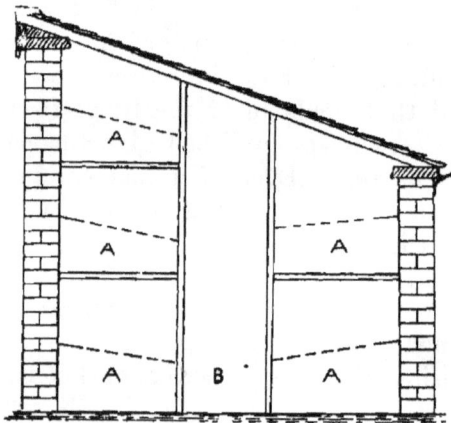

SECTION OF A MUSHROOM HOUSE.

A A Shows the spaces for the shelves on which the beds are formed,
and B The pathway.

and warm in winter. If slates are used there ought to be
a double roof to allow air to circulate between.

As regards the interior, three beds or shelves should be
arranged for at the back and two in front. These shelves
should be 3ft. apart, and each should have an edging 9in. to
12in. deep to hold the manure. The shelves may be con-
structed of wood with slate beds, or entirely of wood. Where
expense is of secondary consideration the beds may be formed
of brick or concrete; in the latter case an iron framework

would have to be used. For all ordinary purposes shelves of stout wood will suffice.

The house should be heated with a flow and return 3in. pipe running around the pathway, the piping being attached to a boiler. A house of this kind is useful for forcing rhubarb and seakale on the floor shelves, and its construction need not be a costly affair. We give herewith a section of such a house. AA shows the beds or shelves, and B the pathway. Where there is no wall available to build a lean-to, then build a span-roof with side walls 6ft. high, under the shade of trees, or where the sun does not shine too powerfully upon the structure in summer. The dotted lines show the slope of the beds when prepared and spawned.

CHAPTER XII.

PESTS AND DISEASES.

Mushroom Pest (Sciara ingenua).—These active little insects often infest mushroom beds, and do considerable injury to the crop.

REMEDIES.—Spray the walls, soil, and floor before spawning with 2½ per cent. of lysol; or dissolve two ounces of salt in a gallon of tepid water, and sprinkle the beds after soiling with this.

Mushroom Disease.—Mushrooms are sometimes attacked in an early period of their growth by a minute parasitic fungus (Hypomyces perniciosus), the mycelium of which develops in the Mushroom and causes the stem to assume a swollen, bulbous-like mass of growth. The infected mushroom consequently fails to grow properly, and the stem

E

eventually changes into a putrid mass emitting a disagreeable smell. The spores of the parasite are no doubt introduced into the mushroom bed with the spawn or the manure.

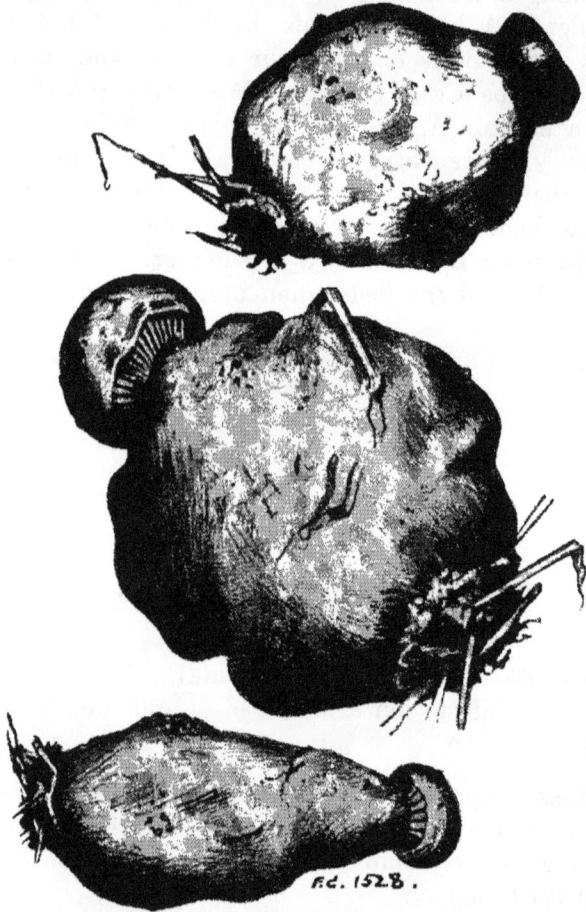

F.C. 1528.

A New Mushroom Disease (Hypomyces perniciosus).

(From Board of Agriculture Leaflet.)

REMEDIES.—Any mushrooms which do not develop properly, or have swollen stems, with scarcely any caps or heads to them, should be removed and burnt. In the case of a severe attack, remove the whole of the manure and soil right away from the neighbourhood of the beds, and then spray the roof, walls and floor of the mushroom house with a solution of one pound of sulphate of copper to fifteen gallons of water. The spraying should be done three times, at intervals of ten days. During this period keep the house warm and moist to encourage the fungi to grow and be more easily killed by the copper solution.

Slugs and Snails.—These are very partial to mushrooms. Trap them by placing heaps of bran or brewer's grains about the beds. Examine the heaps at night, and collect and destroy the slugs or snails found thereon.

Woodlice (Oniscus Armadillo).—These creatures sometimes do a great deal of injury to mushrooms and to the fruits of cucumbers grown in frames. They have also been known to attack young tomato plants.

REMEDIES.—Being night feeders they are difficult to detect. As they congregate when not feeding among rubbish and in crevices of walls and floors, their numbers may be considerably reduced by pouring boiling water on the rubbish and walls. Traps, consisting of dirty flower pots half-filled with moss and laid on their sides, and potato tubers or mangolds with their interiors scooped out, form an excellent means of catching woodlice. Beetle poison spread on bread and butter and laid about the beds will lure them to destruction.

CHAPTER XIII.

COOKING MUSHROOMS.

HAVING been successful in growing mushrooms, it is just as well to know how to cook them to the best advantage. We shall therefore give you a few recipes which we know to be good ones, to enable the housewife to cook mushrooms in the most appetising and least indigestible manner, including also the making of catsup, or ketchup—an excellent sauce, by the way, for use with cold or hot meat.

Stewed Buttons.—Take as many fresh buttons as are required, bearing in mind that a few will go a long way, as they are remarkably rich and substantial when nicely cooked. They must be perfectly clean, and, if necessary, must also be washed. Remove the skin with a cloth, and, of course, cut off the base of the stalk of every one, for that is always gritty. Put them in a stew-pan with a little butter, a pinch of salt, a little lemon juice, and a little broth or gravy. The proportions of these ingredients will, of course, be determined by the bulk of the buttons, and the cook must have some judgment to determine what the proportions shall be. Take care not to overdo it. They must not burn in cooking, and they must not be drowned or over-flavoured. Stew for ten minutes, and serve on hot buttered toast. If it be preferred, the buttons may be sliced, but they are handsomer and better flavoured if cooked whole, unless they are large, in which case slice them the thickness of a crown piece.

Saute of Mushrooms.—Have a few large mushrooms, and take care that they are clean and fresh, for if gritty and damaged they are quite unfit for cooking. Cut off the base of the stem of each, and peel the top. Now smear them all over rather heavily with butter, which may be slightly warmed for the purpose if necessary. Sprinkle both sides with pepper and salt, and lay them stem upwards in a tin dish, and on the stem of each drop a few drops of good sauce. Place them in a hot oven for from ten to twenty minutes, according to their size and the state of the oven. Have ready some rich gravy very slightly flavoured with garlic, by putting in one clove when it is boiling hot

A DISH OF MUSHROOMS READY FOR THE COOK.

and removing that clove in about a minute. Pour the gravy over and serve without toast, unless it be in the form of sippets round the dish.

How to Cook Mushrooms.—This vegetable deserves every care that can be taken to place it on the table elegantly. Its fine flavour and rich fragrance are to be kept in mind, for whatever purpose we intend it, there being always a danger of drowning this out with superfluous

flavourings. Tastes differ in respect of mushrooms, as in
other things—some prefer what are called "fat" and others
"lean" mushrooms. These terms fairly represent the differences observable in them, and no doubt these differences
depend on soil, season, age, cultivation, and so forth. A
fat mushroom is thick-textured and not over large; the flavour is rich and buttery. A lean mushroom is thinner in
texture—in other words, less fleshy, and when full grown
expands to a larger size than a fat one. No matter how or
where they are grown, however, they are all in some degree
fat when young and lean when old, and it is a question for
the cook and the epicure to settle between them what style
of mushroom is to be preferred for any particular purpose.
The smallest buttons of the real Mushroom (Agaricus campestris), are, as everybody knows, delicious if nicely broiled,
but for a prime dish of mushrooms from the grill, whether
to eat alone or with a kidney, or chop, or bacon, some prefer
them fully grown, so that the brown gills are quite exposed;
for in the buttons the gills are hidden by a membrane, which
disappears as the head expands and rends it asunder. Perhaps the most wholesome and enjoyable way to cook full-
grown mushrooms is to put them on the grill, and this brings
us to the first step in practice.

Grilled Mushrooms require a clean gridiron and a
bright, clear fire, with no chance of an atom of dust. The
mushrooms should be fresh and firm. It is usual to wash
them, but this practice is objectionable, for if they are so
gritty as to want washing, it is a fact that water will not
usually wash the grit out. The proper place for gritty and
broken mushrooms is the ketchup jar. We require for the
grill first-rate samples.

In the first place, cut off the stems a little distance from
the gills, so as to remove the gritty root part, and a small
portion of the stem with it. Now gently beat the top to
dislodge any grit that may have got into the gills, and carefully wipe with a dry cloth the top of the cap, but do not
take off the skin unless it is loose. Keep the gridiron cold

BROWN WARTY AGARIC (Agaricus rubescens).

A fairly common species found in woods in Summer and Autumn. (Good for making Ketchup. (See page 68.)

until you really begin to cook. It is usual in all cases to put the gridiron over the fire at once, but our advice to all cooks is to keep it away from the fire until whatever you have to cook is ready to put on. Then your chop or mushroom, or whatever it may be, does not stick and have to be torn off, nor does it get hastily charred instead of cooked by sudden contact with hot iron. Put the mushrooms on stalk-side downwards for a few seconds, and while they are in this position smear a little, very little, butter over the cap; then sprinkle with a little, very little, pepper, and carefully turn them. Now carefully butter them on the under side. If you lodge small pieces of butter next the stems they will quickly melt and flow into the gills, and soften and flavour the flesh right through. Finally dust with pepper and salt, and after about five minutes from first putting them on take them off, put in a hot dish, and have a good look at them, but be quick about it. If not sufficiently buttered and flavoured with pepper and salt you may now add a little more, and at once shut them up in a hot oven to finish. In the course of five minutes they should be ready, and whatever is to be eaten with them should be ready also, for if they are over-much cooked they are considerably spoiled. Above all things, it is necessary to be careful not to overload them with butter or pepper, for they are so substantial in themselves that the strongest stomach may suffer by having to digest much grease and condiments with such meaty diet.

When people are made ill by mushrooms it is fair to assume that the cook is in some part to blame. This is the most wholesome and digestible way to eat mushrooms, and they harmonise with anything from the grill, but especially with a steak or chops or cutlets, and even with toasted bacon or kidneys they make a perfect gustable harmony. The greengrocers' mushrooms are generally good, and for small and casual supplies, such as a moderate household requires, it is cheaper to buy than to grow them.

Pickled Mushrooms.—Buttons may be pickled as follows: Cut off the root portion of the stems and wipe off any soil adhering. Next place some vinegar to which spices as for making catsup have been added in a saucepan, and stand this on the fire until it nearly boils, when add the mushrooms and boil for about three minutes. Remove from the fire and place the buttons in open-mouthed jars, previously warmed, and pour the hot vinegar over them. Leave uncorked for a day or so, add more vinegar, and finally cork tightly. The vinegar should nearly, but not quite, touch the cork. Hermetically seal the cork, and store in the pantry till required. Larger mushrooms in the pink-gill stage only may be cut into pieces, have their skins peeled off, the stalks removed, and then placed in bottles, and have hot spiced vinegar and salt poured over them. Cork and seal as before. Once a bottle is opened in either case the contents should be immediately used.

Mushroom Ketchup.—To each half-bushel of mushrooms add three handfuls of salt. Crush and mix with a wooden spoon. Leave them thus for three days, in the meantime stirring them three times daily. Squeeze the liquor out by means of a cloth, boil it for half an hour, then add six shallots, three cloves of garlic chopped quite small, two ounces each of bruised ginger, whole pepper, and allspice, four ounces of cloves, and a quarter-ounce of mace. After boiling strain off the liquor, and when cool place in pint bottles and hermetically seal.

Mushrooms on Fried Bread.—Choose perfectly fresh mushrooms, peel them and cut off their stems; then fry them partially in butter, add the juice of a lemon, and again fry for a few moments. Next add salt, pepper, and spices to taste, and a spoonful of water in which a clove of garlic has been steeped for half an hour, and again stew till the mushrooms are cooked, when thicken the liquor with yolks of egg, and serve on bread fried in butter.

Mushrooms and Bacon.—Peel some fully-grown mushrooms. Next partially cook some rashers of bacon;

then add the mushrooms and fry slowly. When cooked add
salt and pepper to taste.

Mushroom Soup.—An excellent soup may be prepared as follows : Cut off the stalks and wash the other parts
clean ; then stew them with butter, pepper and salt in some
good stock. When sufficiently tender cut them into small
portions, and boil in good stock added to the liquor they
were stewed in. Serve when sufficiently cooked.

Stewed Mushroom Stems.—The stems of young
fresh mushrooms form a most delicious dish if treated in the
following manner : Wash the stems thoroughly in salt and
water, cut them into thin slices, and then stew them in milk,
adding salt and pepper to taste, also a little butter and
flour. Serve on slices of toast.

Mushroom Soufflé.—Boil some mushrooms in milk,
the quantity to vary with the size of the soufflé basin. Make
a cream sauce with flour, milk, cream, and butter. Add the
mushrooms, which have been chopped in dice. Beat up the
yolks of two eggs (for three persons), add pepper, salt, and
a squeeze of lemon juice. Put into the soufflé basin. Whisk
the whites of the eggs to a snow, lightly stir in, and steam
for three-quarters of an hour. Serve with a table napkin
round the basin, and sprinkle chopped parsley on the top of
the soufflé.

Mushroom Cutlets.—Stew some mushrooms in milk,
to which an ounce of butter has been added. Add a table-
spoonful of grated cheese, a little onion, some savoury herbs,
salt, and pepper. Add the yolk of an egg, and a little corn-
flour to thicken. Turn the mixture out on a floured board.
Shape into cutlets. Egg, and dip in shredded wheat. Fry
in olive oil, drain on paper. Garnish with small sticks of
macaroni to represent a cutlet bone, and decorate each cutlet
with a pink cutlet frill. Serve on a bed of marrowfat peas.
An important point in the frying is to allow the oil to remain

PARASOL AGARIC (Agaricus procerus). [Photo : J. H. Crabtree.

A wholesome fungus found in pastures in Autumn (see p. 67).

on the fire after it has boiled, until its surface is quite still and a faint blue smoke rises. The cutlets should then be laid in, and not before.

Stewed Mushrooms.—Peel the mushrooms, scrape the stalks, and trim the ends. Put the mushrooms into cold water, with a dash of vinegar and a pinch of salt in it. Place in a saucepan one ounce of butter, let it melt, then drain the mushrooms and put them in, adding pepper and salt. Let them simmer in their own juice, covered closely, till tender, adding a little water from time to time should they become too dry. Before serving add a dessertspoonful of flour rubbed down in a little cold water, boil up, and serve very hot.

Mushrooms on Toast.—Proceed as before, and when the mushrooms are drained fry them in a frying-pan with butter or dripping, adding pepper and salt. Toast some slices of bread, cut into rounds, place the fried mushrooms on them, and serve very hot.

Mushrooms and Bacon.—Fry a few rashers of bacon, take them out of the pan, and keep hot in the oven. Put the mushrooms into the pan, prepared as above, and fry till cooked. Serve piled in the centre of the dish with bacon round them.

Mushrooms and Eggs.—Fry the mushrooms as in second recipe, but instead of serving them on the toast poach some eggs and place them on the toast, using the mushrooms as a garnish. If liked, a little thick gravy may be made in the pan and served in a tureen with the three last recipes.

CHAPTER XIV.

EDIBLE FUNGI.

THERE are a number of British fungi which are edible, but, with the exception of the Common Mushroom (Agaricus campestris), it is hardly safe for anyone lacking an intimate knowledge of mycology, and especially familiarity with the genera and species, to gather and eat them. However, we will give a brief description of them.

Common Mushroom (Agaricus campestris).—This is the Common Mushroom of our uplands and meads, and the one to which the cultural data given in this work is applied. Indeed, it is the only kind cultivated. In the earlier stage of its growth it is white, small, and globular; a little later it expands into a convex or flattish cap, with pink gills and a rough brownish-white skin, or epidermis. The gills, too, are not attached to the stem, but to a membraneous ring just clear of it. When fully developed and about to decay the gills assume first a brownish and then change to a blackish tinge. The skin, moreover, readily peels off. In gathering mushrooms in fields only those with pink gills should be taken; then there will be no risk of danger arising through eating them. In a young state mushrooms are distinguished from the mature ones by the name of "buttons." The true Mushroom in nature grows in open pastures or on hilly slopes. Any apparently Common Mushrooms growing under trees or in woods should be strictly avoided.

Horse Mushroom (Agaricus arvensis).—This is a very large species which grows usually in rings in pastures, on roadsides, and in thickets. Specimens of it are recorded as weighing 5lb. 6oz. each, and measuring 43in. in circumference. Another authority affirms that specimens have been seen weighing 14lb. each. Anyway, the species is a monster one. It has a large, flattish cap, a smooth, white, shining skin, grey flesh gills turning to a dark brown when fully developed, and a long white stem. The flavour and smell are strong. This species is employed for making catsup, or ketchup; in fact, it really makes a better-flavoured sauce than the Common Mushroom. It is not safe to eat cooked in the ordinary way.

HORSE MUSHROOM (Agaricus arvensis).
A coarse growing kind used chiefly for making Ketchup.
Found in pastures and thickets.

Champignon, or Scotch Bonnet (Marasmius oreades).—This is the small brownish fungus which usually forms the circles on lawns and in pastures called "fairy rings." As other fungi of a poisonous nature sometimes grow in company with it, caution should be exercised in gathering the true kind. The pileus, or cap, is one to two inches in diameter, fleshy, coriaceous, and wrinkled in texture, convex in shape; skin brownish at first, but ultimately changing to a cream colour; gills of similar colour; stem solid, twisted, and white; and roots attached to the grass. The late Rev. M. J. Berkeley says: "When of a good size and quickly grown it is, perhaps, the best of all fungi for the table, whether carefully fried or stewed with an admixture of finely-minced herbs and a minute portion of garlic. It is at the same time tender and easy of digestion, and when once its use is known and its characteristics ascertained no species may be used with less fear. The French gather this fungus, expose it to the air for two or three days, and then store it in tins for future use. The Champignon will keep in good condition for a long time. The best way to dry them is to thread them together, and when thoroughly dry to store as just suggested. Fungi growing in rings in woods should not be gathered for food."

The Chantarelle (Cantharellus cibarius).—A dainty and delicious fungus formerly held in great esteem as a delicacy at banquets. Not a very common genus, but said to be fairly abundant in Kent and Sussex. The late Dr. Barham tells us in his "Esculent Funguses of England" that "No fungus is more popular than the above, though the merits—nay, the very existence—of such a fungus at home is confined to the Freemasons, who keep the secret! Having collected a quantity at Tunbridge Wells, and given them to the cook to dress, I learnt from the waiter that they were not novelties to him; that, in fact, he had been in the habit of dressing them for years, on state occasions, at the Freemason's Tavern. They were generally fetched, so he said, from the neighbourhood of Chelmsford, and were well paid for." The fungus is of medium size, has its pileus, or cap, lobed and irregular in shape, with a wavy margin. At first the stalk is white and solid, but later becomes hollow and yellow in colour. The colour of the cap is yellow, like that of yolk of egg, and that of the flesh white, with an apricot or plum odour. It usually grows in circles, or segments of a circle, from June to October, in woods or under beech trees. Mr. M. C. Cooke, in his " Easy Account of British Fungi," gives the following recipe for cooking the Chantarelle: "After having picked and washed them, put them into boiling water, stew in fresh butter, a little olive oil, chopped tarragon, pepper, salt, and a little lemon peel. Simmer gently over a slow fire for fifteen to twenty minutes,

[Photo: **J. H. Crabtree.**

CHAMPIGNON, OR "SCOTCH BONNETS" (Marasmius oreades).

The Fairy Ring Mushroom, often seen growing on lawns and in meadows. Gathered and dried they make a delicious dish in Winter.

moisten from time to time with beef gravy or cream, then serve thickened with yolk of egg."

Giant Puff Ball (Lycoperdon giganteum).—This is occasionally met with in gardens, where it often attains the size of a child's head. It also grows in pastures. In a young state it is of a dirty-white colour, changing to brown with age. It is globular or spherical in shape. This species is edible in a young state, when its flesh is quite white; if discoloured it is unsafe to eat. When fully grown the white flesh is displaced by snuff-coloured spores. Epicures eat it when cooked as follows: Cut the puff-ball, whilst its flesh is snow-white, into slices a quarter-inch thick, fry these in fresh butter, and add a sprinkling of powdered herbs, pepper,

[Photo: J. H. Crabtree.

MANED AGARIC (Coprinus comatus).

Known also as the Shaggy-Cap or Ink-Cap fungus. Common in gardens and pastures in Summer and Autumn.

and salt. Another plan is to cut the fungus in slices, peel off the outer skin, dip each slice in a beaten egg, sprinkle with bread crumbs, fry in butter, and add salt and pepper to taste.

Truffle (Tuber æstivum).—This is an underground

F

fungus of a blackish-brown colour, and with a warty skin. It grows chiefly in the Wiltshire, Hampshire, and Kentish downs, and can only be found by dogs or swine specially trained for the purpose. They ascertain by the scent the presence of the fungi beneath, and in this way only can the Truffle be discovered. The Truffle has a peculiar and delicious flavour, which is highly appreciated by gourmets. It is said that the flavour is most pronounced if the truffles are cooked when quite fresh. Truffles are more abundant in the south of France than here; or, at any rate, they are sought for and found in larger quantities than in England. Dried truffles cost from 15s. to 20s. per pound in London. Attempts have been made to cultivate the truffle, but without success.

Morel (Morchella esculentea)—An indigenous fungus growing in orchards and woods during late spring and the early part of summer. We have occasionally received specimens of it from readers of "Amateur Gardening." It grows about 3in. to 4in. high, is of a pale buff colour, and has its pileus or cap indented or broken up with a series of shallow cells. A most delicious fungus, used in a dried state for seasoning, and also in a fresh condition for stewing or converting into catsup, or ketchup. The latter is said to be superior to mushroom ketchup.

St. George's Mushroom (Agaricus gambosus).— This is one of the earliest of our native edible mushrooms, making its appearance about St. George's Day (April 23) in rings on hilly pastures. The pileus, or cap, is thick, fleshy, smooth, soft, and convex at first, developing later into irregular or undulating lobes. The colour is pale yellow, fading to white at the margins; the gills are yellowish-white; and the stem is firm, solid, and white, and bulging at the base. Owing to its early appearance it is hardly possible to make a mistake in gathering, cooking, and eating this fungus. The odour is unusually strong.

Blewits (Agaricus personatus).—A fairly common species

growing in clusters in grass during October. It has a soft, convex, smooth, moist pileus, and a solid, bulbous, lilac-tinted stem. The pileus, moreover, varies from 3in. to 6in. in diameter, and is of a purplish-lilac hue. It must be gathered in dry weather only; in wet weather it becomes soaked with rain, and is unfit to eat. Has a strong odour.

[Photo : J. H. Crabtree.

WHITE FIRWOOD MUSHROOM (Agaricus dealbatus).

A rather pretty fungus, usually found growing in fir plantations in Autumn.

Flesh is said to possess the flavour of veal. Sold largely in Covent Garden for making ketchup.

Parasol Agaric (Agaricus procerus).—A common fungus growing in great abundance in pastures in autumn and occasionally in summer. The pileus, or cap, varies from 4in. to 6in. in width, conical at first, then flat; epidermis

covered with scales, soft, and brownish in colour; flesh white
and cottony; stem long, 6in. or more high, hollow, and bulbous at the base, furnished with scales; gills pale flesh; ring
movable. Possesses a pleasing odour, and is said to be a
most wholesome fungus of delicate flavour. In best condition in a young state. Often sold in Covent Garden Market.

Maned Agaric (Coprinus comatus).—A very common
mushroom, often to be met with in summer and autumn on
roadsides, in pastures, and in gardens. Says Miss Plues:
" It grows in dense clusters, each plant like an attenuated
egg, white and smooth. Presently some exceed the others
in rapidity of growth, and their heads get above the ground,
the stem elongates rapidly, the ring falls loosely around the
stem, the margin of the pileus enlarges, and the oval head
assumes a bell shape; then a faint tint of brown spreads
universally or in blotches over the upper part of the pileus,
and the whiteness of its gills changes to a dull pink. A few
more hours, and the even head of the pileus has split in a
dozen places, the sections curl back, melt out of all form
into an inky fluid, and on the morrow's dawn a black stain
on the ground will be all that remains." It is " singularly
rich, tender, and delicious in flavour," remarks Mr. Worthington G. Smith. Excellent for soups or ketchup.

Brown Warty Agaric (Agaricus rubescens).—This,
also known as the Red-Fleshed Mushroom, is a common fungus in woody places in summer and autumn. Experts consider it a delicately-flavoured and most wholesome kind.
The pileus is convex in shape at first, then expanding flat;
epidermis brown and covered with warts; gills white; flesh
turns sienna-red when bruised; stem hollow and bulbous at
base when old. Has a strong smell. Plentiful in oak woods
in summer and autumn, and makes excellent ketchup.

Clouded Mushroom (Agaricus nebularis).—A not
very common species, with a firm, fragrant flesh which is
much appreciated by epicures. The fungus grows on dead

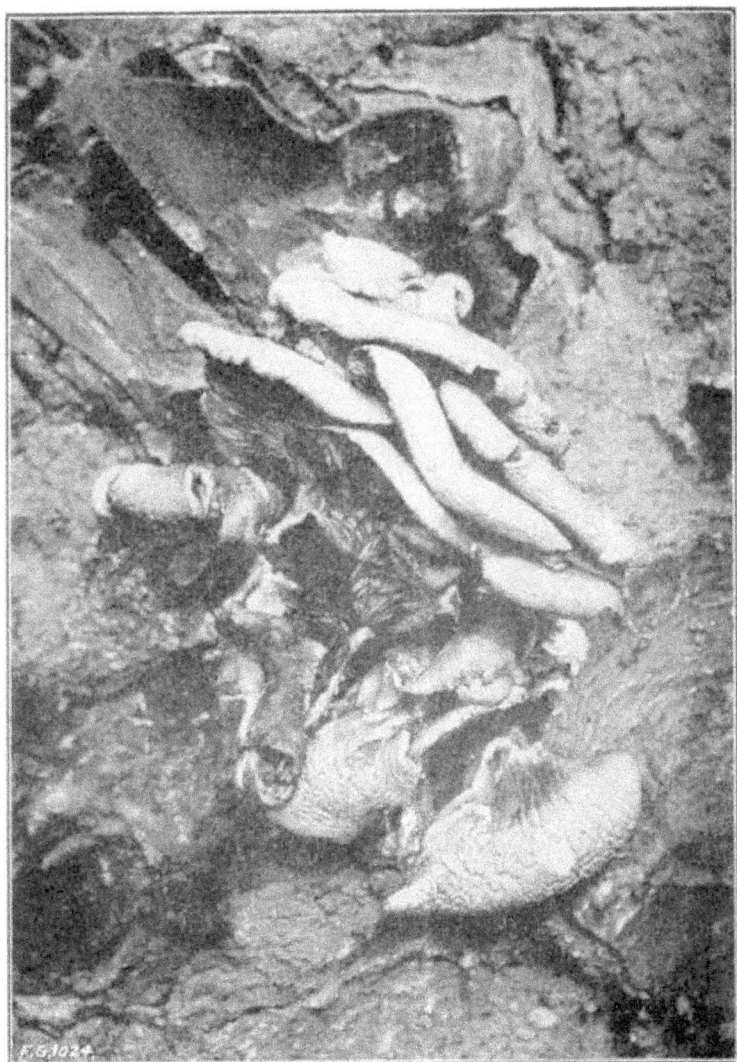

Photo: J. H. Crabtree.

OYSTER MUSHROOM (Agaricus ostreatus).

An oyster-shaped fungus, found growing in Spring, Autumn and Winter
on old tree trunks.

tree leaves in moist places on the margins of woods, and appears late in autumn. The pileus, or cap, is cream or lead coloured, or clouded grey; stem stout, elastic, and striate; gills white or cream, and curving down to and joining with the stem. Odour very powerful.

Orange-milk Mushroom (Lactarius deliciosus).— This fungus may easily be recognised by the orange-coloured milky juice which it exudes on being cut or bruised, and which turns to a green tint after exposure to the air. Fungi which exude yellow or burnt sienna coloured juice should be strictly avoided. The pileus, or cap, is smooth, fleshy, rufous, orange in colour, marked with deeper-coloured zones, and measuring 3in. to 5in. across. Gills yellow and translucent; stem 2in. to 3in. high, solid at first, hollow afterwards, and slightly bent. Grows in plantations of Scotch firs and larches. Said to be a great delicacy.

Viscid White Mushroom (Hygrophorus virgineus). —An extremely common fungus of exquisite flavour. Grows freely on lawns, downs, and pastures in the fall of the year. Easily distinguished by its white waxy appearance. The pileus, or cap, is 1in. to 2in. wide, slightly convex when young and concave when fully grown. Colour, ivory white. The stem is attenuated and tapering downwards. Should be gathered only in a young state. This fungus possesses a disagreeable odour.

Hedgehog Mushroom (Hydnum repandum).—A distinct species, with its pileus, or cap, depressed in the centre and its margins irregularly lobed. The under-surface is furnished with soft, brittle, slanting, awl-shaped spines, which impart to it a distinct appearance. The colour is pale buff, diameter 3in. to 5in.; flesh firm and white, and the stem white, solid, short, and crooked. Grows chiefly in pine and oak woods, and on shady roadsides in autumn. When cooked the flesh has somewhat the flavour of oysters.

Plum Mushroom (Agaricus prunulus).—An excellent fungus which grows in and near woods in autumn, and is highly esteemed by epicures well versed in fungi as food. The pileus, or cap, is fleshy, convex at first and slightly concave later, also irregularly waved at the margin. The dia-

Photo : W. H. Aggett.

THE BEEF STEAK OR LIVER FUNGUS (Fistulina hepatica).

A delicious fungus, which exudes a red juice like that seen in liver or beef steak. Grows on oak or elm trunks in Autumn.

meter is from 2in. to 5in., surface soft, white or grey, and the flesh thick and white. The gills are pink and the stem white, solid, and firm. Odour like that of meal. The flesh is firm, juicy, and of exquisite flavour.

Oyster Mushroom (Agaricus ostreatus).—This fungus grows on the bark of elm, apple, and ash trees in masses or tiers one above the other in spring and late autumn. The pileus is of a dingy or dark hue, as a rule, occasionally whitish or brownish. The flesh is fibrous and firm, and of a savoury nature when cooked. Says Mr. Worthington G. Smith: "A dish of this species stewed before a very hot fire has proved as enjoyable and nourishing as 'a half-pound

[Photo: Mrs. Turnbull.

PRICKLY CAP FUNGUS (Agaricus [Pholiota] squarrosus).

A species found growing in Autumn at the base of ash trees.

of fresh meat.'" It is, however, not one of the most delicious of our native fungi.

Liver Fungus (Fistulina hepatica).—A species which grows on the trunks of old oak trees. It has the appearance of a tongue or piece of liver, and when cut exudes a red juice similar to that seen in uncooked beef or liver. On account of this similarity it is also called the "Vegetable

Beefsteak." Mr. Worthington G. Smith says it grows plentifully on the oaks in Sherwood Forest. Properly cooked it has a delicious flavour.

White Fir-wood Mushroom (Agaricus dealbatus). —A pretty little fungus, with a smooth, ivory-white, wavy, fleshy pileus, and thin white gills which curve round and join the stem. Usually grows in fir plantations, and possesses a delicious flavour when cooked.

[Photo: J. H. Crabtree.

COMMON PUFF BALL (Bovista plumbea).

A fungus easily recognised by its globular ball-like shape.
Common in pastures in Spring, Summer and Autumn.

Edible Tube Mushroom (Boletus edulis).—According to Badham this is a truly delicious fungus, well known to the ancient Romans, and still very popular in Italy. The pileus is 6in. to 7in. across, light brown or bronze in colour; flesh firm and white; stem thick and solid, white at first, then brown, and reticulated. Grows in oak and pine woods, and may be found in abundance in autumn. Mr. Worthington G. Smith, the well-known authority on fungi, says: "Whether boiled, stewed with salt, pepper, and butter, fried or roasted with onions and butter, this species proves itself one of the most delicious and tender objects of food ever submitted to the operation of cooking."

Common Puff-Ball (Bovista plumbea).—This, also known in some books as Lycoperdon plumbeum, is globose in shape, and when fully grown about the size of a walnut. It has a double epidermis, the outer one being whitish and eventually shelling off, while the under one is scaly or warty and of a dull grey colour. It grows in colonies in dryish pastures in spring, summer, and autumn. Gathered in a young state and cooked as advised for Lycoperdon giganteum it is said to be delicious.

Prickly Cap (Agaricus [Pholiota] squarrosus).—This species is shown in the illustration given herewith. Its pileus, or cap, is rough and bristling with dark scales. Grows at the base of ash trees. Is not particularly good flavoured.

Helvella.—A genus of edible fungi possessing an agreeable odour and which may be dried and preserved for use all the year round. Two species are edible. H. crispa has its pileus, or cap, lobed and much contorted, and whitish or flesh coloured; stem hollow, white, and ribbed. H. lacunosa has an inflated, lobed, and darkish pileus, or cap, and a white or dusky ribbed stem. Both grow in woods and on the stumps of old trees in autumn. Excellent for flavouring gravies.

INDEX.

ILLUSTRATIONS.

www.ingramcontent.com/pod-product-compliance
Lightning Source LLC
Chambersburg PA
CBHW021626270326
41931CB00008B/885